Original title:
Frosted Windows, Festive Hearts

Copyright © 2024 Creative Arts Management OÜ
All rights reserved.

Author: Beckett Sinclair
ISBN HARDBACK: 978-9916-90-898-3
ISBN PAPERBACK: 978-9916-90-899-0

Shimmering Echoes in a Frozen Frame

Snowflakes twirl like dancers in a show,
Fumbling mittens dropping, where did they go?
Hot cocoa spills while giggles erupt,
Who knew the snowman could be so corrupt?

Noses red like ripe berries, oh so bright,
Jumping in snowdrifts, oh what a sight!
Sleds go flying, laughter is the tune,
Winter's a circus with a marshmallow moon.

Laughter Dances on Chilly Winds

In scarves too long, we trip and we slip,
But look at that snowman doing a flip!
With cheeks all rosy and spirits high,
We toss snowballs while giggles fly by.

Hot soup warms bellies, but spills on the floor,
Silly cat jumps, and the dog wants more.
Catching snowflakes, tongues out in a race,
Chilly joys painted on every face.

Nurtured Warmth in a Frosty World

Icicles hang like crystal chandeliers,
A snowball fight brings out the cheer!
Slippery pathways, oh, what a mess,
Wipeouts and tumbles lead to great stress.

Chasing each other, the puppy's a blur,
He sneezes at snowflakes and gives a soft purr.
In blankets wrapped tight, we snuggle and play,
These silly moments make bright winter days.

Bright Twinkles through an Icy Lens

Twinkling lights gleam on the snowy ground,
Snow angels are made with laughter all around.
The cat in a hat looks utterly puzzled,
While penguin-shaped cookies become quite the muddle.

Tracks in the snow tell stories untold,
A misfit squirrel looks quite brave and bold.
Hot drinks in hand, we toast to the glee,
In this silly season, let's just let it be!

Glassy Frost

Outside, a chill resides,
While inside warmth abides.
Kids with sleds in spirals race,
In laughter, we find our place.

Mittens mismatched, socks amiss,
Who knew winter could feel like bliss?
Snowmen proudly stand on guard,
With carrots pointed, looking hard.

Hearts Alight

Candles flicker, shadows dance,
Jokes told over hot cocoa's chance.
With marshmallows taking flight,
What a wonderfully silly sight!

Cookie dough flying everywhere,
Flour dusting up the chair.
Giggles echo in the night,
All together, heartbeats light.

Chill Daydreams and Cheery Nights

Under blankets, tales unfold,
With stories of adventures bold.
Furry friends curl by your side,
As giggles and dreams collide.

Ice skating on a dubious pond,
Trips and slips, a goofy bond.
We stumble, laugh, then take a bow,
To winter's whim, we laugh somehow.

Winter's Canvas, Colorful Hearts

With every breath, the air is bright,
While snowflakes dance in pure delight.
Laughter ripples like a stream,
In frosty air, we chase our dream.

Each scarf ties us in a knot,
With tangled stories, chaos caught.
We paint the world with colors bold,
In winter's grip, our hearts unfold.

Crystal Dreams and Festive Schemes

Under twinkling lights we gleam,
Cups raised high, it's a merry scheme.
With gingerbread men on parade,
The sweetest fun that we have made.

Snowball fights and playful shouts,
Chasing around, there's no doubts.
Frosty breath in the frosty air,
With laughter echoing everywhere.

Sparkling Calm with Dance in the Air

In the chill, we gather near,
Laughter mingles with good cheer.
Snowflakes waltz around with grace,
Hot cocoa spills, oh what a place!

Jingle bells and silly hats,
Cats with bows and chubby rats.
We dance like socks upon the floor,
Then trip and fall, yet laugh for more!

Glistening Dreams, Heartfelt Schemes

Under blankets, dreams take flight,
With cookie crumbs, we'll munch all night.
A snowman wears a goofy grin,
His carrot nose is fit to win!

Hot cakes stack, the syrup flows,
Sprinkles tumble, pancake shows.
With every bite, we play a game,
Guess the ghost in pancakes' fame!

Snowy Veils and Inner Fire

Outside, the world is wrapped in white,
Inside, our hearts burn oh so bright.
Tinsel twirls in puppy paws,
Chasing shadows, making jaws!

Mittens fly in friendly brawl,
While snowballs bounce against the wall.
We slip and slide, a merry dance,
Maybe next time, just take a chance!

Frozen Panes and Heart's Delight

Once again, we've lost the track,
Of cookie dough that's piled high stack.
Grandma's laugh fills up the air,
With tales of socks we never wear!

Frosted treats and silly games,
We call out one another's names.
With every giggle and surprise,
We celebrate with heartfelt sighs!

Nurtured by the Chill

Snowflakes swirl like tiny chefs,
Baking chaos on the street.
Cats in jackets, strut like stars,
While dogs just dance on frozen feet.

Sleds become the chariots bold,
Racing down with laughter's cheer.
Hot cocoa spills, a sweet delight,
A marshmallow army, oh so near.

Sparkles on Glassy Shields

Glitter grows on every pane,
Not from elves, but kids at play.
Mittens missing, socks askew,
As the snowflakes join the fray.

Snowmen wobble, hats fall off,
Their carrot noses can't complain.
They wave their arms like funky folks,
In a dance that's snowball insane.

Candles in the Quiet Night

Candles flicker, shadows prance,
As the cat performs ballet.
Pies are warming, scents will tease,
Hungry heads begin to sway.

Fingers sticky with delight,
As cookies vanish—what a sight!
The oven beeps, it's time to eat,
"Just one more," till we're in a fight!

Embracing the Cozy Chill

Wrapped in blankets like a burrito,
Remote controls in hand, we cheer.
The movie's stars are all bizarre,
But we laugh loud, ignoring fear.

Outside howls the frosty wind,
While inside we're warm and snug.
The dance of socks and towering piles,
A living room in a cozy hug.

Brilliant Sparks Through Frosted Glass

In the chilly air, we can feel the cheer,
Laughter erupts as we sip our beer.
Snowflakes dance in a merry swirl,
As kids toss snowballs, oh what a whirl!

Candles alight on the windowsills,
Hot cocoa brews, stacking all the thrills.
Chocolate mustaches on little ones' faces,
While grandma sneaks cookies, no time to erase!

Bittersweet Chill and Joyful Serenade

A snowman's hat is a bit too small,
He wobbles and tips, oh he's bound to fall.
Dog in a scarf, all fuzzy and cute,
But he's off to chase squirrels, oh what a hoot!

Mittens mismatched, a fashion faux pas,
Yet everyone cheers from the warmth of their spa.
Frosty jokes shared, with giggles galore,
While carolers sing, feet tapping on floor!

Windows of Ice, Spirits on Fire

Icicles hang, like nature's bright teeth,
While snowflakes land like confetti beneath.
The radio plays those tunes we adore,
As we play charades, falling on the floor!

Old sweaters worn with a charming flair,
While Uncle Joe dances, without a care.
Spirits are high, like the home-baked pies,
With everyone laughing 'till someone cries!

Snowy Reflections, Luminous Moments

Footprints in snow lead to silent fun,
A family snowball fight just begun.
Sledding down hills, oh what a sight,
With tumbling giggles echoing the night!

Warm hugs exchanged while the cocoa flows,
Who's winning the contest? Nobody knows!
Decorations tangled, lights wrapped around,
As the cat takes a nap on the toy-laden ground!

Luminous Moments

A tree all aglow with ornaments bright,
But it can't seem to stay up straight tonight.
With branches drooping under candy canes,
And silly selfies flood the festive lanes!

Grandpa's lost in the tinsel's embrace,
While grandma's chasing him all over the place.
Joy fills the air, with mischief and cheer,
Let's keep this wild spirit year after year!

Kindlings of Kindness in Cold Air

Tiny snowflakes dance in delight,
Making snowmen with buttoned-up spite.
Hot cocoa spills as laughter erupts,
Whipped cream battles, oh how it jumps!

Scarves wrapped tight, like hugs on a spree,
Sledding down hills, a frosty jubilee.
Chasing the dog who's here for the fun,
He thinks he's a reindeer, on the run!

Winter's Lullaby

The trees wear coats, each branch a quilt,
With squirrels in hats, we can't be guilt.
Snowball fights break out, the stakes are high,
Dodge and weave, or in snow drifts, you lie!

Penguins on ice with quite the show,
They waddle around like they're in a glow.
Fingers so cold, they fumble and slip,
But laughter's the key to keep up the trip!

Hearts Aglow.

With flickering lights in the chilly breeze,
We build up the warmth with love and cheese.
Gifts all wrapped in a style so bright,
Who knew socks could bring such delight!

Carols are sung, off-key with cheer,
As Uncle Joe breaks into a spin near.
The cat's on the table, looking perplexed,
It seems our jolly has her vexed!

Chilled Glass and Warmth Within

The window's a canvas of icy despair,
While inside we bask in the toasty affair.
Grandma's cookies are gold, crisp and sweet,
But watch for the crumbs that dance on your feet!

Marshmallows leap from mugs to the floor,
"Who threw that?" we shout, as we laugh and explore.
Baking attempts that are less than divine,
Yet still, we enjoy with a glass of good wine!

Glimmers of Winter's Embrace

Lights on the roof, they twinkle and flash,
While kids play games and make a mad dash.
Snowflakes the size of a fluffy pie,
No wonder we giggle, oh me, oh my!

A cat in a hat looks quite out of place,
As dog chase his tail with a jubilant grace.
Eggnog spills as toes start to dance,
With all of the joy, who needs a chance!

Laughter in a Crystal Veil

Tiny noses pressed to glass,
Bright snowflakes swirl as we laugh.
A snowman with a carrot smile,
Wearing grandma's hat with style.

Sleds zooming down the snowy hill,
A tumble here, a slip, a thrill.
Hot cocoa spills upon my coat,
The marshmallows cheer, 'We float!'

Twinkling Lights and Cocoa Dreams

Stringing lights on every tree,
The neighbor's cat climbs up, oh gee!
We chase it down, we trip and fall,
While sparkling bulbs sing down the hall.

Cocoa dribbles on my chin,
It's a merry battle to begin.
Whipped cream towers high and proud,
We giggle at our goofy crowd.

Hearts Wrapped in Seasonal Cheer

Sweaters knit with love, they say,
But they scratch and itch, what a fray!
Hats piled high, I cannot see,
Yet still I shout, 'Come dance with me!'

Cookies baked, the sprinkles fly,
Someone's nose is bright and spry.
We share sweet tales of joy and glee,
While tripping over mystery.

Winter's Embrace

Snowmen wear our mismatched hats,
As puppies chase those flying mats.
Icicles hang like toothy grins,
Winter's here, let's all dive in!

Falling flat on icy ground,
With squeals and giggles all around.
The snowball fights are quite the sight,
Bringing laughter through the night.

A Hearthside Tale

By the fire, we roast our snacks,
S'mores galore, we share the facts.
Chocolate sticky on our cheeks,
Everyone's laughing, no one speaks.

Tales of ghosts dance in the flame,
Hot dogs try to hitch a fame.
The cat leaps high, it's quite a show,
As laughter warms us, soft and slow.

Whispers of Winter's Glow

Snowflakes dance on chilly streets,
While squirrels wear their furry fleets.
Hot chocolate spills, oh what a sight,
As marshmallows take their fluffy flight.

Old sweaters hug, there's laughter too,
As we all play peek-a-boo.
The snowman grins with carrots for a nose,
While kids in circles make snowbanks pose.

Reflections in a Chilly Pane

Through the glass, we see the cheer,
As pets bark orders, loud and clear.
Cats in scarves and hats with flair,
Chasing shadows, unaware of despair.

Neighbors juggle gifts with glee,
While wearing mittens, spilling tea.
Baking fails, but who really cares?
As flour clouds become our hairstyles.

Joys Wrapped in Warmth

Cuddle up with blankets tight,
With popcorn popping, what a sight!
We laugh at trips on icy floors,
While warming hands by open doors.

Singing off-key, we raise our voice,
As carolers come without a choice.
The cat escapes, the dog gives chase,
With mistletoe hung in the wrong place.

Glimmers Behind Glass

Icicles hanging from roofs like teeth,
Kids slip-slide with shouts beneath.
Snowball fights in the front yard's glow,
While dad gets stuck in the snow with a toe.

Balloons soar, then pop with a bang,
As one spills cider—what a clang!
The laughter echoes through the night,
As silly poses frame the delight.

Kaleidoscope of Winter Spirit

When snowflakes dance with flirty grace,
We wear our hats, a silly face.
With cocoa cups that warm our hands,
We giggle while we make snow bands.

Outside my door, a snowman waits,
With carrots stuck and wobbly plates.
He seems to grin with icy cheer,
Inviting all to come and steer.

A cat in mittens shimmies by,
He pounces on snowflakes from the sky.
Each chilly gust that swirls around,
Makes giggles bounce on winter ground.

So grab your socks; oh, what a sight,
Our winter games extend the night.
With twinkling lights, so sweet and bright,
We celebrate this frosty plight!

Frosty Breath and Celebratory Beats

With breath like clouds, we sing aloud,
In winter's chill, we feel so proud.
Laughter echoes in frosty air,
As snowmen strut, without a care.

Giggles burst with every slide,
On icy slopes, we take that ride.
Our cheeks are pink, our spirits high,
While snowflakes twirl like apple pie.

Wobbly elves on skates go round,
In the cold, the joy we've found.
Snowballs fly with a playful fling,
We dance, we shout, and brightly sing.

Red-nosed reindeer hopping near,
Whisked by winter's whims—oh dear!
With jingle bells, we stomp our feet,
This chilly chaos can't be beat!

Chills and Thrills of the Season

In cozy socks, we start the fun,
With chilly laughs, we're never done.
Snowflakes falling, bright and bold,
With every flurry, stories told.

We twirl around in scarves so long,
While snowflakes play our favorite song.
Bouncing off the walls with glee,
This winter's chaos suits us free.

Hot cocoa spills, oh what a mess,
With marshmallows dressed in winter's best.
We sneak a taste—and what's the care?
It's always better when we share.

So here's to frosty laughs and cheers,
We cherish these warm, hilarious years.
In every chill, we find delight,
As hearts dance through this winter night!

Crystal Gazing, Heart Fortune Telling

Through sparkling panes our eyes do peek,
Glimpses of magic—how unique!
With fortunes spun in snowy threads,
We find our dreams in winter's beds.

A gnome with spectacles so round,
Whispers secrets from the ground.
He tells our tales through ice and frost,
In giggling tones, no fun is lost.

We toss our wishes on the breeze,
And curl with joy like warming tease.
With every breath, new dreams take flight,
As crystal visions shine so bright.

So let's embrace this wacky view,
Where every whim makes wishes true.
In laughter's glow, we'll spin and sway,
Adventurous hearts outshine the gray!

Shatter the Ice

The air is cold, the laughter loud,
Snowball fights, we draw a crowd.
With mittens thick and noses red,
We build a snowman—the perfect head.

The cocoa's hot, the cookies sweet,
In silly hats, we dance on our feet.
Slipping on ice is quite a sight,
As we giggle and fall with pure delight.

Let Spirits Rise

Dancing near the twinkling lights,
We whirl around and hold on tight.
A penguin suit is quite absurd,
But it's the best laugh we've ever heard.

Mismatched socks and fuzzy shoes,
We trip and stumble, but never lose.
With jingle bells and silly cheer,
We wrap each other in warmth, oh dear!

Holiday Hues Beyond the Chill

Colors bright against the gray,
Sledding down a hill, hooray!
Wearing scarves that are ten feet long,
We belt out tunes that sound all wrong.

A peppermint stick in every cup,
Snowflakes fall and kids erupt.
We try to catch them with our tongue,
And burst out laughing, forever young.

Frosty Frames

Picture frames lined up in rows,
Captured moments in winter's glow.
With goofy grins and snowman pals,
Our memories sparkle, like a thousand galas.

The cat jumps in the latest shot,
Crew's laughter—oh, they forgot!
Shiny bows tangled in our hair,
Fashion fraught with comic fare.

Heartwarming Tales

We sit by the fire, stories unfold,
Of epic fails and adventures bold.
A gingerbread house that fell apart,
Architects? Maybe—we need a restart!

The tales of past mishaps grow funnier,
With every toast, we feel a stir.
The spirit of joy in every ring,
As laughter and warmth make our hearts sing.

Murmurs of the Heart in Winter's Grasp

Whispers shared while snowflakes dance,
In cozy corners we take a chance.
Funny faces made by the fire,
As wacky tales spark our heart's desire.

With marshmallows tossed, we cheer with glee,
No better time than now to be free.
In this funny, warm, and cuddly space,
Hearts are full, all fears we erase.

Chilled Air and Lively Cheers

In the cold of the night, we gather near,
With mugs of hot cocoa and lots of cheer.
A snowman with a hat that's far too wide,
Sips on his drink, what a chilly ride!

Outside it's bitter, but inside it's bright,
We dance in our socks, oh what a sight!
A cat on a table in a cozy sweater,
Tries to catch snowflakes that float like a feather.

A Frame of Frost, A Heart that Glows

Looking out the glass, it's a sparkling show,
With icicles dangling, all twinkly and low.
We throw on our mittens and step in the snow,
And trip over our feet – oh no, where'd it go?

A puppy that tumbles, his ears all askew,
Wags his tail with glee, ready for the view.
With laughter erupting, we look at the mess,
Is winter a joke? We can only guess!

Winter Magic, Echoes of Mirth

The trees wear their coats, fluffy white and round,
While squirrels play tag on the snow-covered ground.
We build forts and tunnels, so grand, oh so wide,
While dodging that snowball a friend launched with pride.

With each gust of wind comes a squeal and a run,
Nobody's stopped by the cold, not one!
Laughter bubbles up as we trip in the ice,
Every slip and every fall has its own silly price.

Glacial Beauty, Flames of Joy

Penguins groove awkwardly, shuffling around,
While snowflakes dance lightly, not making a sound.
We join in the fun with our hats pulled down tight,
Forget all the chores, we'll worry 'til night!

A fire in the hearth, all cracklin' and bright,
We roast little marshmallows, oh what a delight!
With jokes shared around, our spirits take flight,
Who knew winter's chill could feel so full of light?

Heartstrings Wrapped in Light

In the glow of twinkling sights,
We dance like crazy, full of bites.
Mismatched scarves, a sight to see,
Laughter rings like sweet esprit.

Hot cocoa spills, a marshmallow dive,
Who knew joy could so thrive?
Socks that clash and hats askew,
We celebrate the silly too!

Frost Touched

Snowflakes twirl like clumsy ballet,
Wipe a nose, then dash away.
Sledding down a hill, we fly,
With laughter soaring, oh my, oh my!

Laughter echoes 'round the lane,
As we dodge a snowball's reign.
With frozen toes, we toast our cheer,
To winter's whimsy, oh so dear!

Joy Unleashed

The cat wears tinsel like a crown,
A festive furball rolling down.
Cookies piled high, sweet delight,
Who knew sprinkles could start a fight?

We juggle ornaments with flair,
Catching giggles in the air.
Silly socks and jingle bells,
In this chaos, joy compels!

Glacial Frames

Pictures captured in a freeze,
With goofy grins that always tease.
Noses red and cheeks ablaze,
In these frames, we'll spin and craze!

Side by side, we sing off-tune,
Underneath the frosty moon.
Each mishap adds to our tale,
In winter's joy, we shall prevail!

Hopes that Shine

Racquetballs of snow take flight,
As we play till the fall of night.
With snowmen dressed in crazy clothes,
Each new hat, a fresh new pose!

Hot pies cooling, food a'plenty,
Sour faces turn to gentry.
With hearts ablaze, we can't confine,
In this jolly, quirky line!

Chill and Cheer Unite

Beneath the glare of twinkling lights,
We twirl and whirl in bustling flights.
Jingle jumps and holiday games,
With funny screeches and silly names.

Puddles of laughter on the ground,
As weary boots stomp joy around.
Who knew the cold could make us spin,
In this merry chaos, we win!

Whispers of the Season's Glow

The chill arrives with a twinkle and jig,
Noses red, piled high, oh, what a big gig!
Snowmen with scarves that are far too tight,
Waddle and dance in the cold winter light.

Hot cocoa splashes, marshmallows afloat,
While penguins take turns to practice their note.
Laughter erupts with each snowball that flies,
As squirrels in hats do their best to disguise.

Sparkling Pane

The glass is adorned with a shimmery lace,
While grandpa attempts to keep up with the pace.
Tinsel and glitter stuck all on his beard,
He sways to the music, quite oddly cheered.

The cat on the mantle just watches in glee,
As ornaments tumble; oh, what a spree!
Popcorn garlands hang, but fall in a heap,
While munchkins are trying not to fall asleep.

Joyful Soul

With mittens that match and boots gone awol,
A snowball fight breaks out; oh, what a brawl!
Sugarplum visions dance wild in the night,
As children dream up their next great delight.

Grannies in aprons, turning dough into joy,
Tell tales of mischief with cheese and the soy.
While puppies all dig for the treats that they seek,
And Grandma yells, 'No! Just wait till next week!'

Icy Veils

Out in the yard, the snowflakes do flurry,
While Dad sneezes loudly, causing quite a hurry.
A snow fort is built but crumbles with ease,
As kids break for cookies, afraid of a freeze.

The lights are all tangled; oh, what a chore!
As laughter erupts underneath the decor.
Santa gets stuck in the chimney's embrace,
While kids giggle madly; oh, what a place!

Heartfelt Revelries

The smell of pine wafts through halls warm and bright,
While Uncle Joe's sweater looks quite out of sight.
A toast with hot cider, clinks of the mug,
And Auntie finds joy while embroiled in a shrug.

Furry friends bundled in layers galore,
With snowflakes that land – oh! There's even a chore!
They leap with excitement, tails wagging like mad,
In the spirit of warmth, we just can't be sad.

A Shiver of Cheerful Lights

With lanterns aglow, they shine through the night,
As grannies all giggle, all filled up with light.
The cocoa spills over; oh, silly and sweet,
On the floor they're sliding, two left feet compete.

Frost on the ground, we venture outside,
With laughter and joy we can't seem to hide.
Snowflakes can tumble, but we won't miss a beat,
In the whirl of the season, it's jovial and neat.

Mirth Sparkling in the Icy Air

In the cold where giggles bloom,
Hot cocoa floats in cozy room.
Socks dance wildly on the floor,
As snowmen gossip, wanting more.

Children's laughter fills the night,
Snowballs whizz in frosty flight.
A cat in boots struts with pride,
While winter buddies take a ride.

Whimsical hats on every head,
Mittens lost—do they have legs?
Sleds race down the slippery lane,
Who knew snow could cause such pain?

In this chill, smiles brightly stare,
Joy is found within thin air.
With mischief wrapped in snowy cheer,
We dance and play, winter is here!

Choreography of Snowflakes

Snowflakes twirl with tiny grace,
Dancers dash in chilly race.
A penguin slides, says, "Look at me!"
While rabbits hop with purest glee.

Carrots stuck on frosty hats,
Snowballs turn to fluffy mats.
A chorus sings in wintry sleet,
As snowmen dance to rhythmic beat.

Each flake shimmies, takes a turn,
Jokes on lips as cold winds churn.
The ice rink sparkles, twirls abound,
As laughter echoes all around.

Gloves thrown high in playful spree,
Swirling snowflakes lose the spree.
Wipe your nose, don't stop to pout,
The charm of winter brings us out!

Hues of Holiday Bliss

A tangle of lights, a giggle spree,
Cat tangled within, oh, let it be!
Ornaments dance, they spin and twirl,
With cheeky grins and a jolly swirl.

Cookies shaped like funny pals,
Frosting fights and sprinkle brawls.
A reindeer costume, too tight on dad,
Along with laughter that makes us glad!

Snowflakes paint the rooftops white,
While snowman struggles in the night.
His carrot nose, a bit askew,
As neighbors wave and giggle too.

Bright colors flash in chilly air,
Tickled by whims with winter flair.
In hearts aglow, we share our glee,
As this season spins joyfully!

Echoes of Laughter within the Chill

Frosty breaths in the outdoor glow,
Laughter bounces, to and fro.
Boots stomp soft in the snowy cream,
Where winter turns into a dream.

Squirrels scamper, cheeks so round,
With every snowplow mighty sound.
As little kids build forts so grand,
With walls that never seem to stand!

A snowman's grin, a cheeky glance,
While dogs in hats just want to prance.
The joy of slips and playful falls,
Fill the air with cheerful calls.

Under the stars, bundled and bright,
We'll chase the cold with warmth tonight.
Echoes of laughter, hearts ignite,
In chilled embrace, oh what a sight!

Frosted Breath and Hearts Unbound

In winter's grasp, we wear our coats,
Sipping hot cocoa, sounding like goats.
Noses pink, we dance in the snow,
Tripping on ice while the laughter does flow.

Tinsel tangled in our hair,
Who knew gift-wrapping could lead to despair?
Cats in the trees, dogs chasing tails,
All of life's worries aboard the sleigh trails.

Wrapping presents, we get quite the fright,
When last year's fruitcake comes back to bite.
Oh, the joy and the jolly old cheer,
As we toast to mistakes with a... holiday beer!

In hats so large, we can't hear a thing,
Sheepishly blushing as the gags take wing.
Yet with each chuckle, the warmth shows its face,
Celebrating moments of total disgrace.

The Glow Beyond the Chill

Crackling fires with marshmallows high,
S'mores on the menu, oh my, oh my!
Socks on the dog, it's a holiday sight,
Who knew that laughter would sparkle so bright?

Frosty fingers dipped in whipped cream,
Chasing the kids who dream a wild dream.
Fruitcake and cookies divide the room,
One's blissful treat is another's doom.

Giant snowmen dressed in our clothes,
Mismatched mittens and squeaky red bows.
As snowflakes hurl and the warm drinks spill,
We revel in laughter, a joyous thrill!

With jingles and giggles, we sing off-key,
What's this? A cat stuck in the tree?
Through shivers and grins, the heart grows near,
In this wacky chill, we find our cheer.

Chilled Views and Heartfelt Tunes

Fluffy snowflakes dance like a band,
Twirling and whirling, ungainly and grand.
Cuando the hot cider flows like a stream,
We laugh at our antics, a silly daydream.

Sledding downhill, we can't steer worth a dime,
Tumbling like toys, we're just wasting time.
Footprints in snow, a very odd maze,
Follow the trail of our giggling craze.

Hats with bells ringing, scarves flailing wide,
We twirl in the snow with ungraceful pride.
Mittens lost—where did they go?
Stuck under the couch in a monster's abode.

With carols out loud, we scare off the cat,
Wishing the neighbor could play along that.
From the loud, silly songs to a rumble and roll,
Our hearts dance together, warm from the cold.

Celebration Through the Glistening Veil

Candles aglow with unusual flair,
We sit by the fireside, stories to share.
Spicy hot apple cider, a tipple or two,
A toast to the chaos, the fun we pursue.

Tangled in lights, we trip on the mats,
The sound of our laughter, better than chats.
Relatives bickering over who bakes best,
While kids run amok, not caring for rest.

The turkey's a legend, or is it a myth?
It's lost in the oven, but it's making us kith.
Gifts wrapped in paper, just a bit too tight,
Serves as a Frisbee in the heat of the night.

As gifts are unwrapped, we cheer and we groan,
Grandma's hand-knit sweater, now cannot be shown.
With laughter and joy, our hearts never stray,
We celebrate mishaps in the liveliest way!

Glittering Shadows of Kindness

In the frosty air, we see,
A snowman's hat, oh what a spree!
Rabbits hopping, looking bright,
While we giggle at their flight.

Icicles hanging with great flair,
Socks are tangled everywhere!
We sip hot chocolate, such a treat,
And dance around in mismatched feet.

Laughter echoes through the lane,
As sleds go crashing, what a gain!
Snowball fights break out in glee,
The snow is flying, just you see!

Kindness shines like twinkling lights,
Every mishap's full of bites.
So here we sing and play our part,
In joy and laughter, we take heart.

Mellow Duet of Light and Dark

A shadow hops, a giggle's cast,
Where did those bright snowmen blast?
Chasing shadows, we glide soft,
Through the chilled air, hearts aloft.

Mellow jests and playful schemes,
Frosty lips, oh how it beams!
Laughter spills, a joyful song,
In the cold, we can't go wrong.

Candles glow in snowflakes' dance,
With prancing feet, we take our stance.
Mittens flailing, hearts set free,
Together in this chilly spree.

Nighttime cuddles, warmth of cheer,
Chubby penguins drawing near.
In this swirl of light and dark,
We lift our cups, ignite a spark.

Twilight Revelries in Silent Streets

The quiet street, a blanket white,
A cat in boots, what a sight!
Snowflakes fall, the world's asleep,
While we giggle, past the sweep.

With hats askew and scarves a-fly,
We twirl and tumble, oh my, oh my!
Each giggle breaks the wintry hush,
As snowy piles invite our rush.

Twilight sings with playful notes,
As dreamers in their puffy coats.
Through silver light, we spin and weave,
In every breath, we still believe.

Silent cheer, we whisper low,
While skating on the flakes below.
In our hearts, the warmth does swell,
In these moments, all is well.

Frostbitten Memories, Warm Souls

A frosty breath, but hearts are bright,
As kids in boots burst into flight.
Snowflakes biting at our toes,
Laughter blooms with every pose.

We build a fort of dreams and fun,
With giggles rising in the sun.
The chilly air grows warm with cheer,
As fond memories draw near.

Old mittens tangled, lost and found,
Each icy laugh a friendly sound.
The world may freeze; our hearts ignite,
To chase the snow 'til comes the night.

So here's to warmth amidst the cold,
With stories shared and joy retold.
Let's toast with cocoa, raise a cheer,
For every winter holds us near.

Shimmers of Yuletide Joy

Snowflakes dance on noses, oh what a sight,
Woolly hats on everyone, snug and tight.
Carols sung off-key, to laughter we sway,
Merry mischief awaits on this jolly day.

Sipping cocoa with marshmallows piled high,
While pets in the corner, glance up with a sigh.
Tinsel hanging low, a cat's perfect perch,
Pawing at ornaments, a furry church.

Cookies left out for a jolly big lad,
Oh, what a chaos if he snacks like my dad!
We wait through the night, all drowsy and warm,
Then jump at the sound of the night's merry charm.

Twinkling lights adorn the house so bold,
Yet Auntie's dancing leaves us all cold.
A tumble and twirl, we can't help but cheer,
This joyous season, we hold so dear.

A Tapestry of Frosty Whispers

Icicles drip like secrets, a wink from the eaves,
As snowmen hold meetings beneath frozen leaves.
We shoveled the path just to find it again,
While socks on the floor turn our house into zen.

Slipping and sliding, we giggle, we fall,
With mittens entwined like a festive ball.
A chorus of sneezes, presents piled high,
Amidst this delight, who needs to be dry?

The neighbors are peeking, eyes wide with delight,
At our ruckus of joy through the long, starry night.
A feast on the table that's bursting with treats,
While aunties debate on which dessert she eats.

Oh, the tales we'll tell when we glance back in time,
Of faux pas and giggles, of ogling a mime.
Laughter echoes loud, as we gather around,
In this wintery wonder, true joy can be found.

Gathering Warmth Beneath the Snow

Our boots leave impressions, a dance on the ground,
As Grandma's warm cookies gather all around.
The kettle's a-boil, and the chatter's a hum,
While trying to balance the yule log on crumbs.

Pinecones and glitter, we decorate trees,
With laughter exploding like sneezes from bees.
Grandpa's old stories bring smiles and some tears,
As we share all our secrets from yesteryear's cheers.

A hat thrown too high lands atop of the gate,
With bows on our heads, who could ever be late?
The fire's flickering, it sends out a glow,
As we sip from our mugs, with marshmallows in tow.

So let's make a toast, laugh 'til we snort,
To the warmth of this season, our favorite sport!
With giggles and grins, we'll dance through the night,
In this cozy cocoon, everything feels right.

Glazed Perspectives and Cheerful Echoes

Mittens mysterious, mismatched in their style,
A snowy adventure that goes for a mile.
Over hills we tumble, so careful yet spry,
With snowball ambushes and laughter, oh my!

The dog chases shadows, a true winter's knight,
While kids—or are they goats?—leap with delight.
Our noses all rosy, from jumping about,
'Tis the season for giggles—there's never a doubt.

With lights all aglow, the street looks so bright,
As cars drive by slowly, confirming the sight.
The joy in the air is a sight to behold,
With hearts full of laughter, not just of the bold.

So gather your pals, and let the fun start,
With jokes and some pranks, oh, a true work of art!
Embracing this season, let merriment flow,
Laugh heartily, loudly, in this blanket of snow.

Gleaming Cold, Yet Fully Alive

Snowflakes dance upon my nose,
Hiccups laugh, as cold wind blows.
Snowmen wearing scarves too bright,
Chasing sleds with all their might.

Penguins slip and slide around,
Falling over without a sound.
Hot cocoa spills on fuzzy socks,
Joyful chaos, winter's ox.

Birds wear hats, the squirrels giggle,
Ice skating makes my stomach wiggle.
Chattering teeth, I bear the brunt,
Yet here I am, a happy runt.

Icicles form a frozen crown,
Who knew winter could be a clown?
With every breath, I see my puff,
In this chill, I've got enough!

Fables of Warmth Beneath the Chill

Underneath a blanket fort,
We share tales of frostbite court.
A cat in boots, a dog that sings,
Tales of snowmen wearing rings.

Cookies bake and dogs get fat,
Now they're couch kings, fancy that!
Snowball fights that last all day,
Who needs warmth? We're here to play!

With marshmallows like fluffy dreams,
We float away on chocolate streams.
Fables spun from frosty air,
Laughter echoes everywhere.

Giggling friends beneath the quilt,
With chilly tales that we've built.
In every laugh, a bit of cheer,
Who needs spring, when winter's here?

Twinkling Stars Behind Closed Shields

The stars wink from their snowy beds,
While kids make wigs from ice-cold spreads.
Frostened cheeks and laughter breath,
Beneath thick blankets, we jest with zest.

Hot soup spills on mismatched clothes,
Charming stories that everyone knows.
Giggling elves with candy canes,
Building dreams that break the chains.

Curtains drawn, a secret club,
Joking 'bout the winter grub.
With fairy lights just out of reach,
Our joy, not winter, is the speech.

Huddled close, with hearts aglow,
In our bubble, we steal the show.
Beneath the chill, the warmth prevails,
As we tell our silliest tales.

Heartbeats in the Cold Glow

Onward through the frosty night,
We skate with laughter, pure delight.
Snowball showers, quick retreat,
Squeals of joy, let's not admit defeat!

Chilly air brings silly grins,
Wearing socks that never twins.
With hot pies resting on our laps,
Even the laughter gives some claps.

At the fire, the stories roll,
As marshmallows start to toll.
We're not cold, we're living free,
Wrapped in giggles, you and me.

So let the frost do what it may,
We'll turn this cold into a play.
In every heartbeat, warmth we find,
With every joke, our love reminds.

Painted Frost

On nippy panes, a dance of art,
Little hands that giggle and dart.
Rabbits made of sugar and snow,
Leave us grinning with each joyful glow.

The cat does pounce on icy seams,
Chasing shadows, bursting dreams.
While we sip cocoa, marshmallows afloat,
Laughter spills from each tiny coat.

Mittens twirl in a merry array,
As we stumble in heaps, come play,
The chill outside can't freeze our cheer,
With every snicker, warmth draws near.

Joy erupts in winter's embrace,
As giggles echo in this frozen space.
Snowflakes twirl like confetti bright,
Shining through the giggles of winter's night.

Illuminated Souls

Under twinkling lights, our spirit flies,
Dancing shadows and silly sighs.
Eggnog spills from our clumsy hands,
As we wobble on the soft, snowy sands.

Carrots for noses on snowmen proud,
Chasing each other, we laugh out loud.
A mishap here, a fumble there,
Winter's sweetness fills the air.

Snowball fights erupt and gleam,
Covering us in a frosty dream.
We tumble down in giggly piles,
The chilly chaos makes us smile.

Inside we gather, a cheerful bunch,
Talking of snow and a holiday lunch.
With hearts aglow, we raise a cheer,
For laughter everlasting, every year.

Hushed Laughs Behind the Glaze

In chilled silence, a giggle swells,
As we watch our pets with their funny yells.
Hot chocolate spills in a crazy swirl,
While snowflakes twirl, and giggles unfurl.

The dog catches snowballs with puppy glee,
While we hide laughter, not wanting to be seen.
Behind the glass, we snicker and sigh,
Winter's mischief makes time fly by.

Quick little moments wrapped in a freeze,
We smile at blunders, feeling the breeze.
Carrots tip over; hats start to slide,
Our humor melts every icy divide.

As night falls, the laughter stays bright,
A glow of warmth through the shiver of night.
In every chuckle, memories unfold,
Behind that glaze, winter's wonders are told.

Shimmering Night

The moon winks down on a blanket of snow,
As we slip on ice, with a delightful show.
We dance in circles, twirling around,
While our snowman wobbles, nearly falling down.

With every tumble and trip we take,
A chorus of giggles is sure to awake.
We bravely sip cider, though it spills,
The shimmer of joy gives us all the thrills.

A playful snowball sails through the air,
Landing on faces with laughter to share.
Under soft stars, our giggles ignite,
In this charming world of shimmering night.

As we spin tales in the frosty delight,
Each story becomes a new source of light.
So here we huddle, letting joy flow,
While the shimmering night steals the show.

Open Hearts

With scarves tied loud and spirits so bright,
We dash through the park, a comical sight.
Chasing our shadows, with each little leap,
While laughter bubbles, not a moment too deep.

Friends gather 'round in a joyful spree,
With stories and giggles as sweet as can be.
Hot cider spills, and we all shout hooray,
As the world spins 'round in a swirling ballet.

In every moment, we let laughter rain,
Sharing our warmth, ignoring the strain.
With hearts open wide and smiles to share,
We find our joy in the crisp, frosty air.

So join the fun as we ride this wave,
With open hearts, our frowns we save.
Let laughing echoes fill the night sky,
For winter's embrace is a reason to fly.

Icy Borders, Warm Embrace

Ice coats the world, a delicate cover,
But inside our hearts, there's nothing to smother.
With playful nudges and joyful bites,
We build our laughter on wintry nights.

The snowflakes fall, like feathers from dreams,
As we share secrets and whimsical schemes.
In mischief we trade, while giggles abound,
In this wonderland, our joys are found.

Frosted branches, a glittery sight,
While snowmen chuckle in the pale moonlight.
We gather close, in this chilly embrace,
With warmth in our hearts, we find our place.

So even when ice forms its careful walls,
We dance through the night as rapture calls.
For beneath icy borders, our laughter stays,
In the glow of our smiles, winter plays.

Crystals on the Edge of Glee

Tiny snowflakes dance and prance,
As we watch them twirl in a happy trance.
The cat leaps high, but lands with a thud,
While giggles erupt like a warm melting bud.

Hot cocoa spills, a marshmallow lands,
A snowman forms, with wobbly hands.
The dog steals a hat, the kids all shout,
In this frosty wonder, joy is all about.

Winter's Whisper

Snowflakes whisper secrets, cheeky and bright,
While children chase shadows in the pale moonlight.
A squirrel steals a mitten, unaware of the stake,
While laughter erupts with each frosty mistake.

The sleigh ride begins, but the driver's gone numb,
As they wrestle with blankets, giggles become loud hums.

Hot soup's on the stove, with a dash of good cheer,
As snowballs are thrown amidst laughter and beer.

Kindling Warmth

With our gloves mismatched, we brave the cold,
Against pranks of the snow, we're foolishly bold.
A snowball flies, hits the wrong face,
Spreading smiles even in this snowy race.

As the fire crackles, we huddle up tight,
Telling tales of our mischief under the starlight.
A chocolate fountain drowns half the cakes,
While laughter erupts and the giggling wakes.

Frozen Breath

Breathe out your frosty mist with a grin,
As you play hide and seek in the shimmering din.
A sled flies past, with a squeal of delight,
As cheeks turn pink in the cold, starlit night.

Snowflakes land on noses, like tiny soft pets,
While penguins in parkas try to make bets.
The snowman topples, the kids squeal with glee,
In the chill of this magic, we all feel so free.

Radiant Spirits

Fuzzy hats wobble atop our heads,
As we skate like penguins on ice-covered spreads.
A tumble, a roll, laughter fills the space,
As fun takes the lead in this icy race.

Twinkling lights shine on the frosty ground,
With carolers singing, their voices abound.
Mittens lost in snow, a scarf on a tree,
While merry canters dance to our spree.

Silvered Views

Through glass with silver specks, we all peek,
At the dance of snowflakes, so sly and sleek.
While wintertime folly takes center stage,
In our playhouse of snow, we unleash every age.

A snow fort rises, with goofy designs,
Filled with giggles and fun, and questionable signs.
As shadows stretch tall in the dazzling dusk,
The memories we make hold a radiant husk.

Vibrant Beats

With jingles so bright, the night shakes awake,
As we dance in the snow, for fun's playful sake.
The snowflakes clap hands to our silly cheer,
While the chill of the breeze whispers sweet, and near.

Every stumble and tumble just fuels our delight,
As we prance through the snow, hearts glowing so bright.

With hot soup and warm hugs, this season's a treat,
In the comedy of winter, we all find our beat.

Crystalline Dreams of Togetherness

Snowflakes dance on the sill,
Kids with noses bright and chill.
Hot cocoa spills on the floor,
Laughter echoes through the door.

Warm socks lost in the chase,
Who needs style? Just see the grace!
Tinsel stuck in tangled hair,
Jingle bells ringing everywhere.

Stuck indoors, we play charades,
Making faces, new charades!
Gobbles and giggles fill the room,
'Til we burst with forced costume gloom!

We'll toast to spills and silly fun,
With clinking mugs, our hearts are won!
In this cozy, wacky weave,
In each other, we believe.

Embracing the Chill

Frosty air on rosy cheeks,
Snowball fights and sneaky freaks.
Scarves wrapped tight like twisted bows,
Giggles muffled in the snows.

Fluffy hats that flop and sway,
A sweater's hug on chilly play.
Slipping, sliding on ice so slick,
'Til we tumble—what a trick!

Pine trees smell of goof and cheer,
While squirrels plot their squirrelly steer.
Hot pies burn as laughter cranks,
For silly pranks, we give our thanks!

Frolicking in the chilly breeze,
Worries drift like autumn leaves.
Sipping warmth, our hearts set free,
A merry dance for all to see.

Cherishing the Flame

A flickering light in the dark,
Shadows dance with every spark.
Marshmallows pop, a gooey treat,
Smoky faces, oh they can't be beat!

Giggles bubble from the fire,
As tales of ghosts and goblins acquire.
Crickets chirp, a symphony sweet,
While hot dogs roast—oh what a feast!

Fuzzy socks, mismatched flair,
Everyone wrapped in a care to share.
Stay close, dear friends, warmth we claim,
For joy ignites the little flame.

Candles nod, like thoughts of cheer,
In every heart, there's love right here.
As daylight fades, we'll sing away,
Our silly tunes, a bright display.

Holiday Whims in Shimmering Night

Twinkling lights on every street,
Frowning snowmen clutching their heat.
Cookie crumbs line the counter's edge,
While grandpa forgets his own pledge!

Dancing with glee, we spin and twirl,
Muffin caps make our hearts unfurl.
Funny hats that flop and sway,
As laughter bursts—come join the fray!

Snowflakes tumble, a clumsy game,
Each flake is different, how very tame!
Jolly jingles fill the night air,
While cheeky cats plot to snare!

Silly poses for pictures galore,
Facial contortions we can't ignore.
Breezy nights with friends held dear,
In every chuckle, we find our cheer.

Splendor of Season's Embrace

Balloons and laughter fill the room,
Wrapped in chaos, no time for gloom.
Giggles burst with every blow,
As jolly spirits begin to flow.

Slippers that are two sizes too large,
A dance-off ready to take charge!
The tree leans with gifts piled high,
Falling laughter makes us sigh.

Socks that light up, what a sight,
As we prance through the starry night.
Merry chaos reigns supreme,
In this wonderland, we dream!

Hilarity wrapped in golden bows,
A wacky tale only friendship knows.
To celebrate in winks and grins,
With every moment, the joy begins!

Icy Touch

Chilly air kissing my nose,
Jolly boots in matching rows.
Snowmen grinning, hats askew,
Giggling voices shout "It's blue!"

Season's charm with snickers bright,
Hot cocoa spills, but who's contrite?
Fingers frozen, yet we cheer,
As snowflakes dance, we persevere.

Socks mismatched, a wacky trend,
Neighbors laugh, they can't pretend.
Icicles hang, a frosty line,
Winter's script, both odd and fine.

Dancing on ice, we take a spill,
With every fall, we find the thrill.
The cold is here, but so is fun,
Together we laugh, winter's just begun!

Ember's Heart

Through the frost, a spark ignites,
Tickling toes on cozy nights.
Friends gather 'round warm and snug,
Under blankets, we share a hug.

Marshmallows bob, a sweet surprise,
Silly jingles and hearty sighs.
Laughter bubbles, jokes unfold,
Tales of warmth through winter's cold.

Sipping cheer from clumsy mugs,
While snowflakes weave their party hugs.
A cheeky snowball flies askew,
Laughter reigns, it's the best view.

As embers dance, we plot and scheme,
Joy and mischief, what a dream!
With every sneeze and playful bleat,
We find the fun in winter's beat!

Radiant Glow Amidst Glacial Whisper

In the chill, a giggle grows,
While the cold wind playfully blows.
Noses red, like Rudolph's hue,
Each frosty breath, a joke or two.

Lights twinkle like stars on ice,
Gifts wrapped loosely, what a vice!
Unruly ribbons, mishaps galore,
Snow drifts gather, we adore.

Mittens mingle, who's got whose?
Snowball fights, we can't refuse.
With every tumble, laughter flows,
Winter's spirit never slows.

Fluffy hats, oversized and bright,
We twirl and glide, a funny sight.
As we embrace this chilly show,
The warmth within begins to glow!

Winter's Artwork

Nature's canvas, white and clear,
Giggles echo far and near.
Footprints trace a wild dance,
In the snow, we take a chance.

Snow angels draped in silly flair,
With strange designs, we simply dare.
The world is cold, but hearts will shine,
As laughter rings, it feels divine.

Carrot noses, crookedy grins,
Frosty battles, everyone wins.
A flurry of fun, we can't deploy,
Yet somehow, it turns to joy.

Jokes unfold in winter's air,
Tickling senses everywhere.
With every splash and snowy fling,
We sketch our fun, let laughter sing!

Love's Palette

Colors swirl beneath the frost,
In this chill, we find our cost.
Giggles float with every glance,
In the snow, we dare to dance.

Hot pies cooling on the sill,
Winter's warmth, it's quite the thrill.
Mittens tossed, we race and play,
With every step, we swipe away.

Ribbons tangled, laughter loud,
In this joy, we feel so proud.
Crackling fires, a cozy crew,
Love's warm hug, our merry view.

While winter drapes its icy lace,
Inside our hearts, there's just one place.
With frosty fun surrounding us,
We paint our dreams without a fuss!

Festive Dreams on Crystal Canvas

In the chill of a winter's night,
A snowman dances, what a sight!
He spins and twirls with glee and cheer,
Wearing a scarf, he's full of beer!

The frost on glass paints funny scenes,
Reindeer jumping, breaking beans!
Elves in a line trying to sled,
Collapsing with laughter, what a spread!

A hot cocoa mug, I take a sip,
Naughty marshmallows start to slip!
They float like clouds, oh what a treat,
In this frosty world, life's bittersweet!

Snowflakes fall with a giggly sound,
As squirrels frolic all around,
Their tiny acorns, stolen, then tossed,
But oh, here comes winter's merry frost!

Behind the Glass

Peeking out with a silly grin,
Watching the snowball fights begin,
Neighbors bundled up, all aglow,
Chasing cats, oh what a show!

The window fogged with breathy fun,
Little kids play, they've just begun.
A snowball's launched, it flies and hits,
An unsuspecting parent – what a blitz!

Laughter echoes through the night,
As cocoa spills, oh what a sight!
Hot chocolate battles, whipped cream wars,
There's joy for all, and then some more!

Behind the glass, the world is bright,
With silly snowmen in full height.
It's magic made with cheeky glee,
In winter's play, we just feel free!

Light Unleashed

Beneath the street lamps, glows a clue,
A dancing goat, trying to moo!
With ribbons tied in knots and bows,
He prances round on tiny toes!

The lights above begin to twinkle,
While icicles start to giggle and sprinkle.
All animals join, a jolly troop,
They form a conga line, oh what a loop!

A wise old owl with glasses so neat,
Raps a joke that can't be beat.
Snowflakes fall like punchlines true,
Each one laughs as it's born anew!

Under the moon a circus swirls,
With twirling puppies and darting curls.
This season's glow, a joyful dash,
Where laughter lives and moments splash!

Winter's Prism

Look out the window, see what's there,
A dancing bear in his underwear!
Sipping tea with a sneaky grin,
He juggles snowballs, hoping to win!

Colors flash as lights ignite,
A penguin slides with all his might.
Cartwheeling snowflakes join the crew,
In this wild dance, oh who knew?

The snowman plays the slide trombone,
While kids in hats make silly groans.
Toy trains rumble down a track,
Each car is filled with snowball stacks!

As laughter echoes through the night,
Each joyful heart is pure delight.
In this frosty cheer, we find our muse,
Winter's magic is ours to choose!

Joyful Emission

A snowman struggles to stand up right,
His buttons roll in a silly flight.
The birds all chirp with hilarity,
As they watch this snowy parody!

The frost speaks back in a playful tone,
It tells each joke, they're never alone.
With snowflakes giggling, they swirl around,
Creating laughter's joyful sound!

A car spins out, oh what a view!
An old dad slips on the snowy dew.
With a tumble and a flailing arm,
He's greeted by laughter, that's his charm!

Through all the antics, the fun's displayed,
In winter's warmth, no hearts betrayed.
With jokes and stories, friendships grow,
In this wondrous landscape of frosty glow!

Icy Silhouettes

Through crystal panes, a scene unfolds,
A cat in mittens, brave and bold!
She snuggles up to a snowball's might,
Waging war with paws in the night.

Beneath the moon, shadows sway low,
A mouse with a hat gives it a go!
He twirls around on his tiny feet,
In this winter's play, nothing's complete!

A ballet of squirrels makes us laugh,
As they tumble down, they split in half!
Their acorn crowns go flying past,
In winter's show, joy is amassed!

Cold cheeks parade as children sing,
With snowflakes caught on scarves, they cling.
Each icy silhouette finds its place,
In the winter fun, there's endless grace!

Inner Light

Amidst the chill, warm giggles burst,
As cocoa serves its sweetest thirst.
Lights flicker on the tree so bright,
In this cozy room, pure delight!

Outside the door, snowmen plot,
Taking selfies with the family pot.
A puppy joins, his tail a blur,
Posing proudly, he's quite the stir!

Twinkling stars peek through the frost,
While holiday wishes never get lost.
Each heart is full, while laughter rings,
In cozy moments, true joy springs!

From carols sung to playful knocks,
This winter warmth will never box.
In every heart, the light will shine,
As laughter dances, oh how divine!

Milton Keynes UK
Ingram Content Group UK Ltd.
UKHW020039271124
451585UK00012B/932

9 789916 908990